CONCRETE ENOUGH

ANABELLE PINTO

Made with ♥ on the Notion Press Platform

www.notionpress.com

For the ever tumultuous feeling accompanying,

"What comes next?"

Contents

GROUND

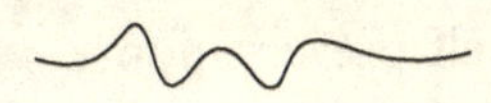

Everything is rushing forward-

Straight at me.

I duck.

I roll myself inward-

A poor attempt at self-preservation-

Waiting to get engulfed and broken.

Like a stick at the shore.

Flotsam and jetsam.

Or,

A beach ball

Tossed around

on unending waves,

Jostled and tangoed

Like an unending dance.

Life is rushing at me

And time seems not to care.

Its nihilistic march

Ignores the things to be done

Leaving lists undone

And tasks uncompleted.

It's not as complicated as it feels

But it's not as simple as they say.

- decisions, decisions, decisions

Life begins to feel

Like an indefinite waiting room

With a ticking time bomb

On the wall.

With the clockface covered

And the heartbeat

Echoes

Through the blank white walls.

I put on today

And it doesn't fit.

It falls loosely at my feet

And I'm unable to carry on

Normally.

Wanting to lay it down

And lay myself down.

Walking the line

Between being awake

And being asleep;

Not able to do anything.

Not able to do what I should.

Not caring about these.

Just waiting for the day to run out,

The sands to run over.

Wishing things undone

would complete themselves.

Praying that this hollow ache

Will fill itself;

Not knowing

How to feel any different.

How do I pick up

And carry this day

That is too big,

Too unending?

Yet even though

it will come to pass

How do I meet the day

It takes me to,

Knowing

I haven't completed yesterday?

The hardest part

of making decisions

is that we don't know

what will happen.

We just don't know.

And that's alright.

(I hope).

It's not admitting defeat.

It's not giving in.

It's simply accepting

I don't know.

5 years from now,

5 months,

5 days,

I do not know

What I'm called to.

But I know where I am now.

I know where I am now

And what this moment

has the potential to be

So, I will be here

And let the future come

Until the *I don't know*'s

Fall

And change into

Here I am.

My parents don't give me the same advice

But they do.

Mama tells me,

"Do it.

Don't think so much.

I don't want you

to live with regrets."

Dada says,

"Think it through.

Don't jump and act.

If you make the wrong move,

You'll regret it."

Don't regret

What will become the past.

You'll carry it around

Like a weight around the ankle,

Chain scratching against the road below.

My parents want me

To live without regret.

Neither from what's done

Or what's left behind.

Don't sleep,

If you haven't put the light off yet.

Sleep,

Even if you haven't put the light off yet.

Sleep peacefully.

Don't let the light disturb you.

My parents give me the same advice.

But they don't.

We're not accustomed to this life yet

A life of waiting while wanting,

Deciding but not knowing,

Searching and searching.

We are not accustomed

To these endless *in between*s,

The *before*s of when life will start again,

The questions and the longing.

It is a difficult time

To wait

As others go on.

Life is moving

While I am still

~here

I'm so tired.

I don't know

What to do anymore.

—

There is nothing to be done.

We're cursed with knowing where we want to be

Before we are ever capable of getting there.

We're getting older,

And the nights

Feel like lifetimes:

Where things are changing,

And as easily as they can slink back,

They are becoming new again.

Home will never feel the same

Cause moving is not a forgettable dance,

And home doesn't stay fixed

In the waters of time.

Sometimes when I ask myself

Why

do I feel like crying?

The answer is-

I

just

do.

We're at the age

Of late nights

And endless days.

Where time is never enough

And there's always

work to be done.

I am sitting here

Dozing,

As the moments meld together.

Nothing

And Everything-

inhaled and exhaled

In the space

Where only sleep is wanted

And nothing can be done.

How many times have you felt like this?

Lost in life

For lack of pursuit?

How many times

Has anxiety perched

Deep in the throat

And high on the brain

Jumping around like a druggie

In withdrawal?

I don't like feeling like this.

Why am I

Unable

To decide

What to do?

~endless crossroads

Loneliness sets in the bones.

A chill that doesn't start or end.

It simply appears

Or is gone;

Awoken on nights

That ask you to hold them.

And nights

Where distance

Is measured in time.

Change doesn't like to sit with me.

It writhes and struggles,

Overwhelming trigger,

Gag reflex.

Change doesn't sit well with me.

It doesn't like my stillness,

My unwillingness to move.

Change moves fast, slow

And unpredictably more.

Sudden slams on the brake.

Whiplash courses down the neck.

Quick slow.

Quick quick slow.

Making up its own dance,

Change moves

Like change doesn't care about the beat,

Like change has its own song.

"How have you been lately?"

I've been thinking about

How a year has gone by

And I didn't think

it would take this long

To find a job.

I've been questioning

What I've been doing?

Why am I still here,

Wasting time?

Even though I've been

Right

Here,

Seeing every decision-

Making every decision.

In such strong judgement

Over the lack of tangible achievement,

Why is it always

The things not done,

Over what has been accomplished?

Why am I

Never good enough

For Me?

The In-Betweens

I lay in bed,

Tired from the nothingness

The blank schedule,

Calendar days

passing by,

with nothing to note.

This is the change.

The bounced email,

Return to sender,

The giant snake

near the finish line

That sends you

Back to the start.

But really,

It simply feels like this-

Like an Erasure.

An erasure of progress,

A moving backwards

When really,

It's just a coming home

A liminal phase

To find what lies beyond.

Disappointment

falls deeply-

Like a shadow

in the setting sun.

It clouds overhead,

Scattering showers,

Billowing in the wind,

Taking the sun hostage.

From shadows

to overcast dullness,

It distorts the world

Like a villain

With ambition.

Disappointment

visits so often,

When trying is in season.

It is at least

A proof of effort.

Proof of hope.

But for now,

The days pass

And nothing feels productive

Except to bring

A *'useless'* feeling,

Even though worth

isn't all that variable.

But it feels so still.

So, I bring on the lists

The unending,

forced *'have to*'s

While I lie

in the in-between

And hope for answers

to, *"What's next?"*

Beyond a shrug

And a practiced,

"I'm figuring it out."

I've been thinking about

The ease of home lately.

Perhaps everything here

Just feels difficult,

Foreign,

Out of reach,

Needed and unneeded.

All at once.

I've been thinking of home

And wishing to go back

But not actually wanting to.

I do not want to go home.

I do not want to stay here.

I simply wish for the easy drawl

Of familiar paths

And spaces to rest,

Weep,

Be anything

And nothing

Whatever way

The wind weathers.

I was drowning in self-pity
While self-criticizing and catastrophizing.

I felt worse,
And worse,
And worse.

"I have so many things to do.
There isn't any time.
I haven't done enough today.
I am not enough for this.
I have a billion opportunities,
A billion responsibilities
And *I am too tired*
And *insufficient.*
I want to go home."

My feelings were not invalid.
They were not irrational.
But they were deeply *sickening.*

I am here.
I am still here.

I am putting one foot in front of the other.

Failing,

Struggling,

Trying,

I cannot reach my own expectations

But I am here

Trying to make it through.

And I'm surrounded

By unending love

And the support of many hands

And many voices.

The day after Christmas

I am alone again

And there's nothing to be done.

Everyone home, has gone out.

I am left to watch the dogs

And eat my dinner

In however much silence I make,

And see the lights twinkle

In the house next door

While music streams out in loud mouthfuls

Along the chilly night-time breeze.

There is nothing else.

~Longing and waiting.

They lied.

Memory lane isn't a calm stroll,

Nostalgia dripping off

Every lamppost,

Every train.

Like the aftermath

Of a warm rain

That hugs the trees

And everything

Until it is ready to hit the ground;

Long after the clouds have passed.

Memory lane

Is a slippery slope

Filled with walks under a shared umbrella

And cold breezes

You can't shake out of a sweater.

Memories that passed like a hug-

Too quickly,

Warmth lasting only a while

Before the cold comes rushing back.

Too soon.

There's a quiet solitude to going back

while everything rushes forward

In the wild brake of time;

Reaching a hand backwards

Against the steady currents:

Wild,

Maddening,

Undeterred.

Let me fall down this slippery slope

Into the arms of a friendly ghost,

Hoping only for the touch of a memory

That might serve to warm

Like warmth once did.

LEVEL

My feet are bricks.

My mind a maze.

My heart a weight,

Stomach a pit.

I feel as though

I'm walking myself down

A deafening silence.

Into an unnerving nightmare.

Like I will be all alone.

All over again.

Adjusting is hard.

Knowing it is a struggle

Makes it harder.

A p p r e h e n s i o n.

I am a twig

Dangling off

A magnificent birch,

The wind is strong

And I am bound to go

Much farther

Than the apple falls.

My feet are bricks.

My mind a maze.

I am moving again,

And adjusting's a curse.

We all have pictures of ourselves
From when we were younger
We'd like to forget about.
But our parents have
Put them up on the fridge
Like they were our best moments.

And they'll stare back at us
With childlike innocence,
Questioning,
"Why don't you like me better
If *you* are *me?*"

And we'll say uncomfortably in reply,
"I don't know.
I just don't feel confident
About the way I looked when I was *you.*"

Sad, defeated,
Where does your lack of confidence come from
If not from the little girl you told,
"You're not pretty."

I think the hardest thing

About leaving

Is an empty hand

Never feels as cold,

As after it learns w a r m t h.

"I'm sorry

I can't remember

Even if I've asked before."

The kind of forgetting

That runs so deep

It's weightless.

It doesn't know

If the question

Was ever asked.

It's thrown away

By time,

Was it?

Perhaps it never existed.

Not here,

Not like this.

It is familiar

Just not from encounter.

~ Why does forgetting feel so wrong?

It doesn't make you

inconsequential to me.

It's just that

our memories find home

in different kinds of shelters.

Not all was brick and stone.

I'm sorry there's a *weight* in my chest and a *hole* in my
stomach

They said it would be different.
They said
I would find my heart carved out,
Empty and bleeding
And my stomach a pit
Endless and weeping.
But it's not the same.
It's not the same.

I'm sorry.
There's a *weight* in my chest
And a *hole* in my stomach.
You're gone
And I'm not there anymore.
Everything that's existed
Is written off,
Like secrets
Only the ground knows for sure.

I'm surviving on supplements and prayers.

Some days you can't fend off loneliness

So you sit with it.

Head pounding.

Eyes tired, brimming.

Everything else-

E m p t y .

I listen to music

Trying to find a way;

Stave it off,

Keep it at bay.

But here I am still

Sitting with loneliness,

Not sure how

To tell it to

Stop following me.

I have problems

With things

No one else has problems with.

In these strange new multiverses

Of life changed without me

I do not know

What these new realities contain.

For when I had left,

Their light

Nor shadow

Existed or forecast.

I do not know

These new dimensions,

These people,

These boundaries

That have come up

And washed away.

I do not know anymore

How to live my life

In its calm daily stupor,

Cause it's now in motion

And I haven't had the chance

To count myself in

Before jumping into

The double dutch.

Reclamation

We carved out shelter from the rubble;

Crafted from chaos.

Lived in walls that weren't our own,

Painted then,

& Found ways to respire

in the bounds of suffocating inheritance.

Looked out,

And searched within.

Rebuilding,

Recreating,

Pulling out space

from under oceans of lost sand.

Filling up bottles with

Space and time,

And slowly making space

Where there was once

Nothing

But emptiness.

Reclaiming spaces

That now bear our names

And hold our lives.

Reclamation is a hefty task.
How do you tell the walls closing in,
"You are not keeping me trapped.
You are shelter and safety" ?

We've made new homes
From the rubble,
And our safety
Within these make-shift shelters
Feels stolen
By changes
That happen
while we sleep.

Even development
feels a curse
To the comfort of home
Begotten.

These walls don't feel
Like the home I'm used to.

These changes have overtaken

My known habits,

The spaces I meld with,

The ones I have made.

Change feels like a robber in the night,

Stealing comfort reclaimed

Redecorating what was mine

Like an unwelcome rebranding effort.

My expectations usurped.

My memory polluted.

My comfort dethroned.

So, once again

with these walls around me

It's time again

To retrain their meaning

And reclaim a life that's mine.

I've been revisiting old friends

Expecting them to see

How much I've changed,

How much I've grown.

But I hear the rusty old adage,

'It's like nothing has changed.

You're the same as before."

And something within me

Twings and twangs

Like an almost erasure

At the lack of validation.

But perhaps, it's not that I've changed really

But that I've grown more

Into the person I already was

Becoming.

And now, I've simply learnt

What decisions I'd make

In new and different surroundings.

In new and different ways of being.

We've been brought up

On hormone grown chickens,

On ideas of big and bold beauty,

On taking what you want

And being e v e r y t h i n g .

Why does life feel so heavy?

~ a prayer

Raincheck

It's raining.

You message me.

We talk about how fast it came on,

How quickly it left,

Why I had to miss it.

When it'll come back.

It's raining again.

I message you

Before you have the chance to reply.

I'm walking in the rain

Letting cold sweep in

And goosebumps rise.

It's raining now.

I thought of messaging you.

But forgot.

You're not here anymore.

You won't know the difference.

It's raining.

It's cold.

It's stopped now.

I wonder,

Will it rain again?

What are we doing here?

Will you let me know when you find out?

Or is there something

In the wondering,

In the unknowing

That ignorance might actually be bliss.

But what if I am simply lost?

Along the pointer I align the stars.

But *I don't know what home is.*

Maybe I have walked past it,

Or circled round,

Or fogged up the glass with my breath,

Looking in.

I don't know what I am doing

But I know I am here.

If you figure it out,

Will you let me know?

Or is our existentialism unique?

If you find out,

Will you let me know?

I am either lost at sea,

Or at the bottom

Of an empty well.

But still,

I am d r o w n i n g .

We don't get anywhere,

Holding onto our mistakes.

But we go nowhere

Without them.

I smell of sweat and bad weather,

Tiredness

And bad luck.

Like the wind has blown by,

Wet mud kicked up by the rain

And everything everything

Can never stand and wait.

What do you do with a failed relationship?

Do you hold it awhile, saying
"You tried your best,
It wasn't your fault"?

Do you push it into storage
Along with all the things
That take up too much space,
So that it'll be *easier* to live?

Do you mourn it
As though it died,
Some sort of disease
Diagnosed too late,
That it passed too early?

What do you do?
There is so much hurt.
There is so much attachment.
There was too much hurt to stay
And there is hurt to leave too.

Do you try to revive it

Regardless of how little you trust it

To breathe on its own?

Regardless of how many times

You have tried to make it better,

Kept all the medicine ready,

Filled the water bottles,

Sat with tea and kanji,

And yet it has refused,

Said *there's nothing to be done.*

But even if you accept the failure,

And rationalise that blame helps nothing,

How do you abandon it

And move on?

What do you do with a failed relationship

Besides try to forget about it,

And hopefully heal from it?

Do not erase your culture from your words.

Do not ask your hands
Why they have failed
To hold onto
All the things they have let go.

Do not ask your mind
Why it has not
Remembered,
Your heart
What it has failed
To know.

Do not ask your hands
Why they have failed
To hold on
To culture,
And knowledge
And handed on things.

What you have is enough.
Do not forget it,
But do not question yourself over it.

Your hands have let go
That your feet may move forward
Lest you stay stuck in place,
Stop the days from passing on,
The sun from setting,
Stick yourself
Knee deep in questions.

Do not ask your hands why they've failed
While they are still holding you up;
While they have picked you up
When you've fallen;
While they have wiped tears away
And handled everything
That's come their way.

Do not ask your hands
Why they have failed,
Nor your heart,
Nor your mind.

They have not failed you.

PLAN

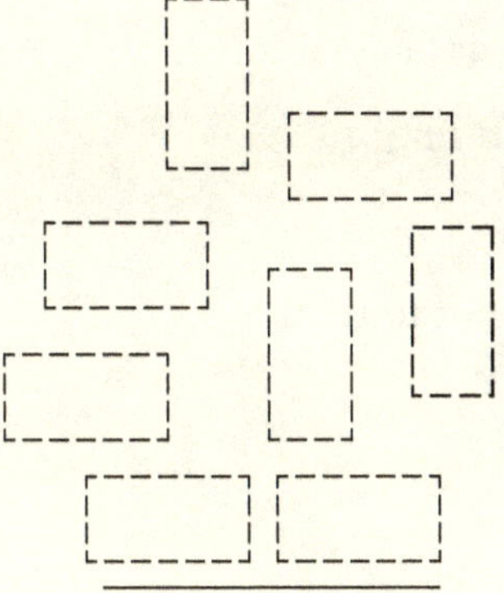

When we think of things

We know we can't have

It leaves us **a c h i n g .**

It's the same with people.

When we think of those

We can't have near us,

It leaves us **a c h i n g .**

That's why I try not to think

Too long

About *you.*

I stop myself

From mulling over

The *what could've beens*

And the *if onlys,*

Because it leaves me

With happy dreams

That are **cold** in their ending.

I love you.

I miss you.

When home feels too far away,

Call.

When times feels so long,

Message.

And when you're able to

Come back.

Come back.

They never tell you

How much it pains

To be an individual.

It's always
Freeing,
Wild,
Independence.

But never
L o n e l y,
S t r u g g l e,
R e s p o n s i b l e.

Responsible carries more,
Heavy,
Weighing,
Tense.

We are always individual

But we need not remain alone.

~ Community

Seen

Known

Loved

We never had such ambition.

We didn't want to be CEOs

Or anything much.

We wished for slower days

With sunset gilded afternoons.

A dog on a porch,

The cool gentle breeze

And enough space

To love and breathe.

And not much else

But strength in our joints

And the song in our souls

To carry us on

And stay as long as they could.

Sometimes we know ourselves

Too intimately

To believe

We are capable.

Sometimes we feel like

We are our feelings

To believe

We are capable.

Sometimes we get tired

Of talking to our concerns

That we believe

They are capable.

Sometimes we forget

About the world around us

That we become

Our own world.

Sometimes we get too familiar

With ourselves

That we forget

to listen.

Sometimes we feel

We know ourselves

Too intimately

That we don't listen,

And can't believe

We are capable.

> *~Putting together what sometimes adds up to*
>
> *The sum of sometimes*

There are more days than this.

Do you crawl into bed

Wishing the days

Weren't so loud

In their criticism?

Do you wake up heavy

Wishing the sun would take longer

To be back in front of you?

Do you stay up all night

Wishing the quiet spaces

Would swallow you whole

In their safeness?

There are days beyond this.

There are days that will bring you back.

Days that will say:

The night isn't over,

Even though tomorrow has arrived.

Days that ask:

A little more sleep,

A little more care,

A lot more gentle kindness.

Days that brighten

And lighten.

That find you feeling not as heavy,

At least not as much.

People who will see you.

See You-

As you are.

There is love

That is non-romantic,

Non traumatic,

Non tiring and unobliging.

Actual love

That will tell you:

You are enough.

If ever it had a measurement,

You are more than worth

The space you take,

The air you breathe,

The time you spend.

There will be days

That feel more difficult

Than anything

You could have ever imagined

Without being anything great.

There can be blood in the water

Without giant waves,

And sharks with pointy teeth.

There are days

When giving up

Is a sweet dream

And nothingness sounds

Impossibly kind.

Yet,

There are more days than this.

I'm sorry

For the hard days,

The impossible ones

That make you feel

Lesser,

That make you feel

Unbearably worthless.

I'm sorry

I don't know how to make it all go away.

But there is more.

It'll take time.

But as certain as these days feel,

Change is even more certain still.

Feelings will change.

Days will pass.

There is more still

For

You.

We forget to imagine

The struggle

that comes with big change.

We skip over it

And jump right into the

Good parts-

Where life is adjusted,

Routine is set in

And familiarity is built up.

Until we stand at the precipice of big change

And feel the dips and heights

That astound and terrify,

Without any way to ease into

The bones of a new life.

Having to put it on

And adjust while you walk

For a while in these new found shoes.

"Perfection isn't needed."

The problem was
I didn't believe you.

I didn't believe that
You really meant it.
I was meant to be perfect,
I had already learnt it.
That that was what was
Valued,
Admired,
Desirable.
That that was what was expected of me.
A 10 out of 10
A perfect score.
A neatly pressed uniform.
To arrive in class on time,
Not a second late.
That forgetting my sports uniform,
My sports shoes
Was fine,
As long as my grades were high.

That that was all that mattered.

Nobody cared that I was quiet

Or didn't have so many friends.

Nobody cared that it was uncomfortable

To be expected to be

A natural leader,

An excellent speaker,

A helpful student

Meant to improve others' performance.

That noise was a deterrent

That creativity was meant only in the prescribed

channels,

During arts and craft

Or composition

That everything had it's supposed

*Meant to be*s

And I was meant to be

P e r f e c t .

To speak well,

To study well,

To adapt well,

To be helpful.

And serious.

And kind.

And talented.

What wasn't important faded away.

Practice makes perfect.

A practiced smile

At the right moment.

Even if you don't know

A simple nod

An easy agreement

I'm not sure where the idea came in

Perhaps it didn't.

It was never pushed onto me-

It was just all the rules.

There was never any pressure to be perfect

But always the expectation that I would be,

And that was enough.

Today, I pray

that the silence

will find me more willing.

That in every empty space,

every moment

that I look back on saying,

"In that time,

I could've…"

I will also remember

that these were opportunities to rest,

release

regroup

and remember:

That there is more to life than striving.

There is more

than what today describes.

There is after

and evermore.

And even if I'm standing still

or stopping,

my toes are yet pointed

in a good direction.

Hope and healing

Are a crazy expanse

of rollercoaster.

One that's under construction,

With walks in between,

Hard hat zones

And lines to wait behind.

BUILD

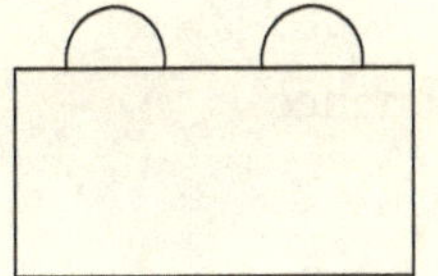

I "love" how it seems

That every feeling requires

Permission

To sit easy.

How every new experience

Enters with new mixtures

Or feelings in feelings

And every expectation

To go smoothly.

But

It's *normal*

For things to go wrong,

Or mistakes to happen.

N o r m a l

Is an unrelenting warmth

That comforts the new,

The uncertain.

But bears heavily

Once normal

Becomes normal,

And change is no longer

A foreseeable turn.

You can start over

As many times as you like;

As many times

as there are cities and people.

You can start over;

Begin.

Again-

Accepting that a new life

Does away with the old,

Or reviving

Some long forgotten

Old part of you

You like to credit better days to.

And yet,

again and again

Try and fail.

You can start again.

Who taught you to fear like this?!

This was not born with you.

Nor written into your blood.

Fear is learnt

Through careful recitation,

Through painful instruction

And unfortunate experience.

Stories that caution

And anxiety that curls

Who taught you to fear

So readily?

So eagerly

So undoubtedly

That you can doubt stability

But not that which fear determines.

Life is a constant updation

Of the things

That we have seen,

Know are possible,

Attempt

And then are able to accomplish.

Sometimes the journey is smooth.

Sometimes it is littered with longevity.

But more than that,

It just is.

Always.

~Law of conservation of mass

I am committing myself

To being a thief-

A thief of all the beautiful things in this world

That I do not have the pride

Over such invention

So instead,

I shall steal away

the small beauties

Conceived in the hearts

Of those whose love overflows

onto their loved ones

In prayers and warmth,

And blissful action.

That speaks volumes to poetry

And rewrites the great sonnets

Only to be breathed out

Like an undying breath of life.

I am stealing ways of love

That blend into life

As an ever-instilling

Jar of hope

Of the good of humanity,

The great of love,

The best of us.

And I hope

That like many a plant

My Grandmother has grown

With a smile and a twinkle

Such will grow best

As stolen plants often do.

~of stolen plants & love

Wherever I go,

I am blessed

that I have people to love while I'm there,

and people I'll miss when I leave.

A dusty port town
On the edge of bustling
It's future noisy.
But the now,
The now is quiet seaside.

Dusty port town
That stretches afore
The water front
And holds its breath
But then let's out
A shaky exhale
On waves that ebb and flow
As busy turns busier
But for now stays stuck
In the quiet port town
Too big to stay too quiet.
So let's enjoy it,
Drink in the calm longitude
While the day still lasts.

Today is asleep

And tomorrow is dreaming,

Walking through fields of dreams

And snoozing in the poppies.

Goodnight.

Good morning.

Sweet dreams.

Fair morrow.

Early riser,

Fly.

You are not meant to stay

Unshatteringly still.

It will only keep you warm

And teach you *This is safe.*

But safety is not ironclad.

It is not unchanging.

It is not stagnancy.

Safety beats to its own dynamic.

Safety finds a light

Even 'midst a transitioning sky.

Safety walks

And runs,

And flies.

And safety doesn't know how long it will stay;

And neither do you.

So you cling to where it's been before,

That safety's footprints

Stay longer in the sand.

As sand slips away

And things start to change

Safety seems distant.

But safety has simply changed.

But it is still

P r o t e c t i n g you.

I wonder if this life

Is a repetition

Of before

Or when they tried

And failed

To make me understand

What this part

Could ever mean.

Whether moral, metaphor

Or allegory,

I've begun

Again

And again,

Yet I fail to learn

The lesson this life is writing.

"Allowed"

They say

We're allowed to do this,

We're not allowed others.

We're falling in between

Cracks and spaces.

Allowed.

Must.

Mandatory.

Disallowed.

Must not.

Prohibited.

We are the checks and balances

The ethics

And justification

We are no longer people

We are simply

Tokens

Of what we could do.

Of who we could be.

But only within

The lines that they draw

We are stuck.

"Allowed."

Lest solely trespassing.

I don't want to think of the what ifs .
The days that tell us
what could have been.

What if he loved me?

What if I missed the alarm?

What if she didn't have to leave?
What if she didn't want to?
What if she didn't ?

What does it matter
If *if* could be?
Is wouldn't.

Can I hold your hand
And tell you
It's alright?
That the days will not end here

Could is a strong word.

It holds potential in its mouth

Like a gun at its trigger.

We run down long streets

And winding roads

Clicking heels on the sidewalk

And passing by street-lit spots.

There is a turn to every sentence,

A thrum to every heartbeat.

A curiosity,

A challenge.

Could be.

Can do.

Try.

Let's.

We can't do everything in this small life,

But we try our hardest.

There's still time

I would like to be in love.

To dance and let everything fade away,

To laugh early in the morning

Or on a sunny afternoon.

I'd like to stand side by side

In the kitchen,

In a grocery store parking lot,

In the waiting room of many a hospital,

PTA,

And in all the heavy moments.

I would like to share silence,

And warmth,

Worries

And woes.

I would like to not be afraid

Of the consequences of my words

But only say as much as I can;

How much I love you;

How much I appreciate you;

Without holding back,

Without forgetting.,

I would like to meet you

To see you even when it's raining,

Or snowing,

Or hailing.

To meet you when the sun

Is bearing down on us.

To eat ice cream in every weather

And spend long days together.

To talk about everything.

To help each other.

To bring out the best

And leave spaces for rest.

I'd like to relax in your presence

And share faith,

belief

and love.

I feel so young and so old

All at once.

Like I haven't yet learned

How to shop

For clothes for a night out.

Or choose

The right place

To buy vegetables.

Or find the right timing

To speak my mind

Without feeling like

An overflowing dam.

I don't know how

To step out in the world

And say *this is my best.*

I should be here.

I am ready.

I am worth it.

I do not yet know

How to be confident

In who I am

And what I want.

Or perhaps

I just don't know

These answers yet.

We do not leave 22 behind

when we take on 23.

Every year of your life

is equally as important

as the ones before,

and the ones to come.

There may be things

to leave behind

and things to cling onto,

But 23 doesn't forget 22,

It simply

Adds to it.

Whisper it into the dark unkindness of late night
solitude,
When nothing feels like home
And the days are neverending.
Whisper it when the birds are about to fly
And you have more than one goodbye to meet.
Whisper it when there is nothing wrong,
But a single wave
Deep down below
That feels like a hurricane looming.
Whisper it to me
And I'll whisper it to you.

~it will be okay

I don't know what to tell you, love.

Life is difficult.

It gets crazy

And then it gets really quiet.

It gets confusing

And winding

And sometimes,

I don't even know how I feel.

Life is difficult...

But there are moments

Of softness,

Of gentleness,

Of quiet clarity,

Of laughter over conversation

And *relation*

That feels real

And genuine

And easy.

Life can be easy too.

So what should I say.

Is it difficult,

Is it hard?

Is it easy,

Is it comforting?

Life is like this, love

You can say everything about it

And you'll never be wrong.

You can say anything about it

But you won't always be right.

Life is a many faced die

It rolls

And you don't know

Where it might land.

I don't just live with the present.
The past locks arms with me
As I walk down familiar roads.
It hides behind me,
Dragging its feet down new parades.
The past has separation anxiety
That's difficult to placate.

The present is always ongoing,
Witnessing everything
before turning to past.
It's always changing.
It's always here.
But it never stays.

The future looms ahead,
Day by day .
Asking me questions,
Trying to make plans.
The future asks me of myself
Where I'd like to be,
Who I want to be,
Who I'd like to stay with.

I don't just live with the present

In its changing days,

Its flux,

Its drama.

The past hangs around

While the future lies in wait.

The road is rugged,

Noisy,

Unrelenting.

To the bucket list I never knew I needed

To being a terrible recipient of surprises
And complaining to my mom
About unexpected goodness.

To being the last ones
In a restaurant that's waiting
To switch off the lights,
But aren't rushing you off too much.

To long nights that turn into
Unexpected viewings
Of the sunrise,
Breakfast before the day's rest.

To changing the bedsheets
During summer afternoons
And sleeping through the daylight.

To buying flowers
On a random day
And converting an old bottle
Into a temporary home.

To rushing back before curfew
In an auto converted to
Rollercoaster on unfixed roads.

To spontaneous plans
To order in.

To late night walks
Post dinner
On fairy like corners.

To piling up
Glasses of chai
That eventually fall
like the tower of Babel
On a cloud hung evening.

To late nights spent
Talking on couches
And under buildings,
Along empty roads,
And illegal chai stalls.

Concrete enough

You are meant

For much more.

You are meant

for much more

than *maybe* plans

and uncertain love.

You are meant

for more than just

Enough

Or *excuses*.

You are meant

for more that

late night texts

And forced pageantry.

You are meant

for whole-heartedness

And unfailing kindness.

You are meant

for more than what

this world advertises-

The whirlwind romance

That burns out

as fast as it started;

The constant competition

and the chase for success;

The physical focus

That ignores the softness of the soul.

You are meant for much more than this.